Hamster Escape

by Conor McIntyre
illustrated by Trish Hill

SCHOOL PUBLISHERS

Copyright © by Harcourt, Inc.

All rights reserved. No part of this publication may be reproduced or transmitted in any form or by any means, electronic or mechanical, including photocopy, recording, or any information storage and retrieval system, without permission in writing from the publisher.

Requests for permission to make copies of any part of the work should be addressed to School Permissions and Copyrights, Harcourt, Inc., 6277 Sea Harbor Drive, Orlando, Florida 32887-6777. Fax: 407-345-2418.

HARCOURT and the Harcourt Logo are trademarks of Harcourt, Inc., registered in the United States of America and/or other jurisdictions.

Printed in China

ISBN 10: 0-15-350418-8
ISBN 13: 978-0-15-350418-1

Ordering Options
ISBN 10: 0-15-350332-7 (Grade 2 Below-Level Collection)
ISBN 13: 978-0-15-350332-0 (Grade 2 Below-Level Collection)
ISBN 10: 0-15-357439-9 (package of 5)
ISBN 13: 978-0-15-357439-9 (package of 5)

If you have received these materials as examination copies free of charge, Harcourt School Publishers retains title to the materials and they may not be resold. Resale of examination copies is strictly prohibited and is illegal.

Possession of this publication in print format does not entitle users to convert this publication, or any portion of it, into electronic format.

4 5 6 7 8 9 10   985   15 14 13 12 11 10 09 08

Jenna was taking Fudge, the class hamster, home for the holidays. "Don't let Fudge out of his cage," said Mrs. José, the teacher. "He might escape."

Jenna took Fudge home on the school bus.
"That's a nice pet," said the young woman from the apartment above.

"He can run on a wheel. He can wash himself, too," said Jenna.

Jenna went into her apartment.
"Look, Mom!" said Jenna. "Fudge is home for the holidays."

Jenna was excited to have Fudge at her house. She opened the cage door to see Fudge better.

Suddenly, Fudge ran out of the cage.
In seconds, he had disappeared
under the couch.

"Oh, no!" cried Jenna. "Mrs. José said to leave Fudge in his cage!"
"We will find him," said Mom.

They hunted for Fudge in the plants.
They looked behind the curtains.
They even looked inside Jenna's
blue shoes.

It was tough finding Fudge! Finally, Mom looked in her purse.
"Fudge!" said Mom.

"There you are!" said Jenna. She held Fudge carefully against her.

Jenna put Fudge back in his cage.
"You won't open his door again,
will you?" asked Mom.

"Never!" said Jenna. "I'll leave Fudge safely in his house. I promise!"

Think Critically

1. What were the three places that Jenna and Mom looked for Fudge before they found him?

2. How do you think Jenna felt when Mom found Fudge?

3. Would you like to have a pet hamster? Why or why not?

4. How did Fudge get lost?

5. How can you tell that this is a fiction book?

 Social Studies

Draw Diagrams Fudge was missing in Jenna's apartment. Draw a map of a room in your home and label all the places where a hamster might hide.

School-Home Connection Tell a family member about the story. Look around your home and discuss all the different places a hamster could hide.

Word Count: 199